The Countries

Northern Ireland

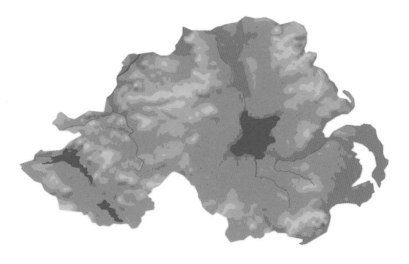

Tamara L. Britton
ABDO Publishing Company

**visit us at
www.abdopub.com**

Published by ABDO Publishing Company, 4940 Viking Drive, Edina, Minnesota 55435.
Copyright © 2004 by Abdo Consulting Group, Inc. International copyrights reserved in
all countries. No part of this book may be reproduced in any form without written
permission from the publisher.

Printed in the United States.

Photo Credits: Corbis pp. 5, 6, 8, 9, 10, 11, 13, 16, 18, 19, 21, 22, 24, 25, 26, 27, 29, 31,
    33, 35, 36, 37; Getty Images pp. 30, 34

Editors: Kate A. Conley, Stephanie Hedlund, Kristianne E. Vieregger
Art Direction & Maps: Neil Klinepier

Library of Congress Cataloging-in-Publication Data

Britton, Tamara L., 1963-
    Northern Ireland / Tamara L. Britton.
        p. cm. -- (The countries)
    Includes index.
        ISBN 1-59197-296-5
        1. Northern Ireland--Juvenile literature. I. Title. II. Series.

    DA990.U46B665 2003
    941.6--dc21

                                                                2003044315

Contents

Hello!

Hello from Northern Ireland! Northern Ireland is on an island in the North Atlantic Ocean. Its land has rugged mountains, as well as beautiful lakes and valleys. The country is also home to many plants and animals.

Northern Ireland is part of the **United Kingdom**. It shares the island of Ireland with the independent Republic of Ireland. Many Northern Irish people think the countries should be united. But, others want the two nations to remain separate. This disagreement has caused much violence.

Despite these troubles, many countries are working to help Northern Ireland create a government that represents all its people. Northern Ireland's people are working hard to make their nation safe and prosperous.

Hello from Northern Ireland!

Fast Facts

OFFICIAL NAME: Northern Ireland
CAPITAL: Belfast

LAND
- Area: 5,452 square miles (14,121 sq km)
- Mountain Ranges: Mourne Mountains, Sperrin Mountains, Mountains of Antrim
- Highest Point: Slieve Donard at 2,796 feet (852 m)
- Lowest Point: The Marsh at -1.3 feet (-.4 m)
- Major River: River Bann
- Major Lake: Lough Neagh

PEOPLE
- Population: 1,685,267 (April 2001 est.)
- Major Cities: Belfast, Londonderry
- Languages: English, Irish Gaelic
- Religions: Protestantism, Catholicism

GOVERNMENT
- Form: Constitutional monarchy
- Head of State: Monarch
- Head of Government: Prime minister
- Legislature: Parliament
- Nationhood: 1920

ECONOMY
- Agricultural Products: Cattle, hogs, poultry, eggs, dairy products; potatoes, barley, hay, apples, pears, plums
- Mining Products: Chalk, clay, limestone, gravel
- Manufactured Products: Fine china, processed foods, Irish linens, aircraft, automobile parts, electronics
- Money: Pound (1 pound = 100 pence)

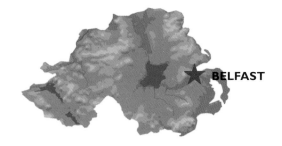

Northern Ireland's flag

Northern Ireland's money

Timeline

700s	Several clans live on the island of Ireland
1100s	Normans invade the land
1607	English Protestants begin settling Northern Ireland
1641	Irish rise against the English settlers
1689	William III becomes king
1690	Battle of the Boyne
1801	Act of Union
1920	Government of Ireland Act creates Northern Ireland
1949	Republic of Ireland separates from the United Kingdom
1968-1969	Violence in Northern Ireland grows
1985	Anglo-Irish Agreement
1994	Cease-fire between Irish and British
1998	Peace agreement reached
2000-present	Peace agreement is suspended and resumed several times

History

In the 700s, different Irish clans ruled Ireland. In the 1100s, **Normans** invaded the island. Many Irish moved away after the Normans took over.

King Henry VIII

In 1541, King Henry VIII of England became king of Ireland, too. England's people became **Protestant** during the **Reformation**. Despite this, most of Ireland's people remained **Catholic**.

In 1607, James I was king of England. He gave Irish land to Protestant settlers from England and Scotland. These new settlers spread the Protestant faith. Soon, more English Protestants settled in northern Ireland.

This upset Irish Catholics in southern Ireland. Not only had the Protestants taken Irish land, but they were also **discriminating** against Catholics. So in 1641, the

Dunluce Castle was built around 1300. Today, it is a popular tourist attraction.

The people of Northern Ireland agreed to this act. Southern Ireland, however, did not agree. It wanted one undivided nation that was free from all British rule.

In 1921, leaders from southern Ireland signed a treaty that created the Irish Free State. It went on to adopt its own constitution. Then in 1949, it formed the Republic of Ireland and became completely independent of the **United Kingdom**.

Northern Ireland, on the other hand, was still part of the **United Kingdom**. Distrust and hatred between **Protestants** and **Catholics** were strong. This led to years of conflict.

In 1968 and 1969, civil disturbances between Protestants and Catholics were violent. The Irish Republican Army (IRA) began **terrorist** bombings in Northern Ireland to advance the cause of a unified Ireland.

In 1972, Britain suspended Northern Ireland's **parliament** and ruled the country from London. Then in 1985, the United Kingdom and Republic of Ireland signed the Anglo-Irish Agreement. It allowed the Republic of Ireland to have a voice in Northern Ireland's government.

Neither Northern Ireland's people nor the IRA liked this agreement. Throughout the 1980s and 1990s, the IRA terrorized Northern Ireland and Britain with bombs. So, Protestant groups responded with more violence.

The British-Irish Council is a group of representatives from several different countries that meets in an effort for peace.

A 1994 **cease-fire** was short lived, and the bombings continued in 1996. In 1997, formal peace discussions began between all parties involved. The talks ended in 1998.

Voters in Northern Ireland and the Republic of Ireland approved measures to bring peace to their nations. But today, Northern Ireland is still unstable. The 1998 peace agreement has been suspended several times. The region's leaders, however, are still working to bring peace to Northern Ireland.

Land

Northern Ireland is on the northern end of the island of Ireland. It shares the island with the Republic of Ireland. The Irish Sea separates Northern Ireland from England. The North Channel separates Northern Ireland from Scotland.

Lough Neagh (lahk-NAY) is in the center of the country. It covers 153 square miles (396 sq km). It is Ireland's largest body of water. It is also the **United Kingdom**'s biggest lake. Northern Ireland surrounds the lake, like a big bowl. Around the bowl's rim are the country's highlands.

The country's highest peak is Slieve Donard (sleev-DAHN-uhrd) at 2,796 feet (852 m). It is in the Mourne Mountains, which run along the southeast coast. The Sperrin Mountains rise in the northwest and the Mountains of Antrim ring the northeast.

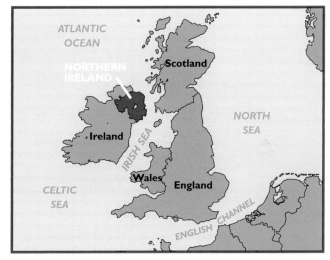

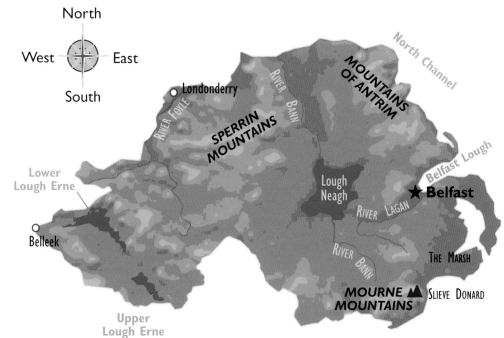

Northern Ireland's longest river is the River Bann. It starts as the Upper Bann in the Mourne Mountains and flows into Lough Neagh. Then it continues from the lake as the Lower Bann, and flows to the Atlantic Ocean.

Northern Ireland has hundreds of miles of beautiful coastline. The country's coast has many bays and harbors. Dozens of lakes, rivers, and streams add to the natural beauty of the country.

Northern Ireland also has large areas called **bogs**. The bogs have acidic soil. This has preserved **artifacts** from the past, such as pottery and wooden items.

Northern Ireland has a mild climate. The temperature ranges from 35° Fahrenheit (2°C) in the winter, to 65° Fahrenheit (18°C) in the summer. However, Northern Ireland can be both windy and rainy.

The Mourne Mountains have many rich pastures around them.

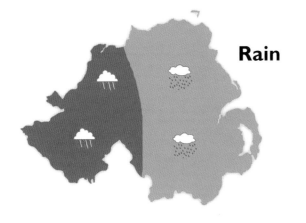

Rain

Rainfall

AVERAGE YEARLY RAINFALL

Inches		*Centimeters*
Under 20		*Under 51*
20 - 40		*51 - 102*
Over 40		*Over 102*

North

West — East

South

Winter

Temperature

AVERAGE TEMPERATURE

Fahrenheit		*Celsius*
Over 65°		*Over 18°*
54° - 65°		*12° - 18°*
43° - 54°		*6° - 12°*
32° - 43°		*0° - 6°*
Below 32°		*Below 0°*

Summer

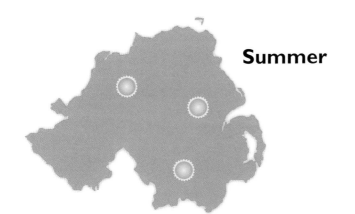

Plants & Animals

Thousands of years ago, Northern Ireland's land was covered with forests. But as the population increased, people cut down the trees to clear land for farms. They also needed wood to build ships.

Today, only about 5 percent of Northern Ireland has forests. Most of the nation's trees have recently been planted and are still young. They grow on plantations.

Because of destruction to their natural **habitat**, most of the country's animal life is small. However, red, fallow, and sika deer live in Northern Ireland. They live in the country's remaining forests.

Forests and lakes are part of the beautiful scenery found in Northern Ireland.

Many species of birds live in Northern Ireland. Some pass the winter there and then migrate in the summer. Others live there all year. Geese and swans winter in Lough Neagh. Seabirds, such as puffins and kittiwakes, live along the coast.

Northern Ireland has around 40 natural reserves. These areas preserve the country's natural environment. And, they provide **habitats** for wildlife.

Swans in Northern Ireland

Northern Ireland's People

Northern Ireland's people come from different areas. Many **descend** from ancient Irish peoples, such as the Celts (KELTS). Others descend from settlers who came to Ireland from England and Scotland. Still others come from different parts of the world.

Religion divides the people. About half of the people are **Protestant**. The rest are **Catholic** or follow other religions. English is Northern Ireland's official language. People also speak Irish Gaelic (GAY-lihk), the language of Ireland.

Most people live in cities, such as Londonderry or Belfast. About one-third of the country's population lives in rural areas.

Most families eat meals of meat, potatoes, vegetables, and bread. As in most British countries, tea is Northern Ireland's most popular drink.

Families in Northern Ireland often celebrate holidays and other special times together.

Irish students

After breakfast, children go off to school. Children are required to attend school from ages four to 16. First, they go to primary school. When they are 11, some attend secondary school. There, they receive **vocational** training.

Others go to grammar school, where they take university preparatory courses. Still others attend comprehensive school. There, students learn both secondary and grammar school subjects.

Students who have completed the required education may attend one of Northern Ireland's two universities. They are Queen's University of Belfast and the University of Ulster, which has four **campuses** throughout the country.

When they have completed their education, Northern Ireland's people get jobs. They work in the nation's service, manufacturing, and agricultural industries.

Boxty

Boxty is a tasty Northern Irish dish similar to potato pancakes. It is usually served as a side dish with meat.

- 1/2 pound cooked potatoes
- 1/2 pound grated, raw potatoes
- 2 cups flour
- 1 teaspoon baking soda
- 1/2 teaspoon salt
- 1 cup buttermilk
- oil for frying

Mash cooked potatoes and place in large bowl. Mix grated potatoes, flour, baking soda, and salt into mashed potatoes. Gradually mix in buttermilk. Add oil to skillet and heat. Drop one large spoonful of batter into skillet. Cook over medium heat until boxty is light brown on both sides and a little puffy. Remove from skillet. Continue with remaining batter.

AN IMPORTANT NOTE TO THE CHEF: Always have an adult help with the preparation and cooking of food. Never use kitchen utensils or appliances without adult permission and supervision.

English	Irish Gaelic
Hello	Dia dhuit (JEE-a GICH)
Good-bye	Slán (SLAWN)
I am sorry	Tá brán orm (TAW BRAWN ORAM)
Mother	Máthair (MAW-hir)
Thank you	Go raibh maith agat (GO RAV MAH A-gat)
Friend	Cara (KAHR-a)

LANGUAGE

Economy

Most of Northern Ireland's people work in service industries. They work in education, government, banking, health care, and trade.

Others work in manufacturing. Northern Ireland is famous for its fine linens. In the village of Belleek, workers make china that is treasured all over the world. Other manufactured goods include processed foods, automobile parts, and computer chips.

Northern Ireland has many deepwater ports. So, workers manufacture ships in the nation's shipyards. Workers build warships, ocean liners, and tank ships.

Making linens by hand is an old method, but it is treasured by many people.

Some of the nation's people work in agriculture. Farmers raise cattle, hogs, and poultry. In turn, they produce meats, eggs, and dairy products. They also grow potatoes, barley, hay, apples, pears, and plums. Fishers catch cod, mackerel, herring, shrimp, salmon, and trout.

Several fishers in Northern Ireland use nets such as these to catch the day's supply of fish.

Cities

Belfast is Northern Ireland's capital and largest city. About 300,000 people live there. It is located on the River Lagan and is a center of trade, service, and education. Its people make ships, processed foods, and **textiles**.

The famous British ship *Titanic* was built in Belfast. Belfast is also home to Queen's University, which was founded in 1845.

The **Titanic** *under construction*

Londonderry is Northern Ireland's second-largest city. It has around 100,000 people. Londonderry is often called Derry for short. It lies along the west bank of the River Foyle. The city's main industries include tanning and linen making. It is also a center of trade with other cities in the **United Kingdom**.

Queen's University in Belfast

Traveling & Talking

Northern Ireland has an excellent system of roads. All of the country is accessible through this system. The nation's ports process much freight, and **ferries** carry people to different cities.

The government-operated Northern Ireland Transport Holding Company controls the railways. Rail systems link the country's major towns. They also link Northern Ireland with cities in the Republic of Ireland, such as Dublin.

Passengers can choose from three airports in Northern Ireland. The Belfast International Airport provides service to major international cities.

Northern Ireland has three major newspapers. The country receives broadcast television service from the British Broadcasting Corporation. Ulster Television provides local programming.

Railways in Northern Ireland carry both people and supplies all over the island.

Government

Northern Ireland is part of the **United Kingdom**. Its government is a **constitutional monarchy**. The United Kingdom's monarch is the head of state. The British **prime minister** is the head of government.

The country's laws are made by the United Kingdom's **parliament**. Parliament is made up of the House of Commons, the House of Lords, and the monarch. The House of Commons has 659 members. Northern Ireland's people elect 18 of them.

The 1998 peace settlement created the Northern Ireland **Assembly**, the North-South Ministerial Council, and the British-Irish Council. The assembly has 108 members, elected by Northern Ireland's citizens.

Queen Elizabeth II has been the United Kingdom's monarch since 1952.

The North-South Ministerial Council has representatives from both Northern Ireland and the Republic of Ireland. The British-Irish Council represents the Republic of Ireland and the **United Kingdom**.

Locally, the Northern Ireland Office runs the government. The **secretary of state** for Northern Ireland runs the office. Northern Ireland's land is divided into 26 districts. The citizens of each district elect a council. Its members serve four-year terms.

Belfast's city hall

Celebrate!

Holidays in Northern Ireland are called public holidays. Northern Irish celebrate all of the **United Kingdom**'s holidays.

July 12 is a public holiday called the Twelfth. On this day, a **Protestant** group called the Orange Order marches in parades. The group is celebrating King William III's victory over King James II in the Battle of the Boyne.

A **Catholic** organization, the Ancient Order of the Hibernians (AOH), also holds marches during the year. Two of the AOH marches celebrate the Feast of the Assumption on August 15 and Saint Patrick's Day on March 17.

Northern Ireland's most famous festival is the International Arts Festival. It is held each November at Queen's University of Belfast. Festival goers enjoy music recitals, plays, art shows, lectures, and movies.

These boys are protesting Protestant parades that go through their neighborhood without permission.

Leisure Time

Northern Ireland's people have many ways to relax. They watch television and go to movies. Often, they visit friends at a local public house, or pub. There, they can have something to eat or drink and listen to music.

In Northern Ireland, soccer is called football.

Many people play on sports teams. Watching sporting events is also a popular activity. The country's most popular sport is soccer. People also enjoy **cricket** and **rugby**.

Walking is a popular activity in Northern Ireland. Ulster Way is a 560-mile (901-km) footpath around the country's six counties. Walkers enjoy a wide range of scenery including coastal views, lakeside valleys, and beautiful mountains.

Students in Northern Ireland visit a museum for a class trip.

Northern Ireland has an Arts Council. It promotes appreciation of the arts. The Ulster Orchestra performs in Belfast. Belfast is also home to other famous orchestras.

Ulster Museum is the country's national museum. It is located in Belfast near the Botanic Gardens. It has many fine displays of Northern Irish history, natural history, and arts.

The Ulster Folk and Transport Museum is a huge museum filled with information on Northern Ireland's history. It has reconstructed old churches, schools, and cottages. It also includes displays of early carriages, bicycles, and aircraft. It has a large display of cars and trains.

Left and opposite page: The Ulster Folk and Transport Museum has both old and new forms of transportation on display.

Northern Ireland is a beautiful country with rich **cultural** and natural resources. Its troubled past has caused many people to move away. It has also kept many people from visiting the country. But, the government is working hard to bring all of Ireland's people together, so they may finally live in peace.

Glossary

artifact - a useful object made by human skill a long time ago.

assembly - a group of government officials that makes and discusses laws.

bog - wet, spongy ground made up of decayed plant material.

campus - the grounds and buildings of a school, university, or college.

Catholic - the Christian church under the authority of the pope.

cease-fire - a suspension of hostile activities.

constitutional monarchy - a form of government ruled by a monarch who must follow the laws of a constitution.

cricket - an English outdoor game played by two teams of 11 players. They use a ball, two bats, and two wickets.

culture - the customs, arts, and tools of a nation or people at a certain time.

descend - to come from a particular ancestor or group of ancestors.

discrimination - unfair treatment based on factors such as a person's race, religion, or gender.

ferry - a boat used to carry people, goods, and vehicles across a body of water.

habitat - a place where a living thing is naturally found.

Normans - Vikings who settled in France. They and their descendants went on to conquer parts of Italy, England, Wales, and Ireland.

parliament - the highest lawmaking body of some governments.
prime minister - the highest-ranked member of some governments.
Protestant - a Christian who does not belong to the Catholic Church.
Reformation - a religious movement in the sixteenth century. People who wanted to reform the Catholic Church formed Protestantism by making these changes.
rugby - a form of football played with an oval ball by two, 15-person teams.
secretary of state - a member of a leader's cabinet who handles relations with other countries.
terrorism - the use of terror, violence, or threats to frighten people into action.
textiles - of or having to do with the designing, manufacturing, or producing of woven fabrics.
United Kingdom - the united countries of England, Scotland, Wales, and Northern Ireland.
vocational - relating to training in a skill or trade to be pursued as a career.

Web Sites

To learn more about Northern Ireland, visit ABDO Publishing Company on the World Wide Web at **www.abdopub.com**. Web sites about Northern Ireland are featured on our Book Links page. These links are routinely monitored and updated to provide the most current information available.

Index